Scribbling on Blank Canvas

Collection of Poems

Kanika Agarwal

Published by:
Sahityapedia Publishing
Noida, India – 201301
www.sahityapedia.com
Contact - +91-9618066119, publish@sahityapedia.com

First Edition - 2022
ISBN - 978-93-91470-22-7

Stories are all around us. Like the air, the story embraces us. We are living one and narrating another.

Stories are a medium to escape. Like a time machine, a story transports us. We are escaping one and lost in another.

Stories are yours. Like a blank canvas, a story lets you paint anything. We are thinking one and painting another.

CONTENTS

* * *

In Depths

Do you understand the word "love" which you say so surely?
Being a sentient being, we feel, we think, we act, we co-habitat,
Share our depths in those late-night messages only to hope we understand,
Can't those unspoken words by reading be deceived?
Or are we able to talk in the language which we only can perceive?

Unless spoken out loud, you have no way to know what you have conveyed.
Now there's a choice – write or say? Be angry and cry or be accommodating?
Both the paths can either be a bliss or be a crack in the glass.
You think back on the word "love" hoping it could give you the clue,
But the word itself is as clueless as it could be for you to decipher.

Unconditional – that's what I have listened to experts saying,
But who's to say they have mastered the level of zen?
One word can't encapsulate the depths of it,
Surfing such unchartered territories people don't have names,
They get hurt, they care, they laugh, they cry, they die.

If you think that you have uncovered those secrets,
If you think that you have proved it to be "the one"

Then how could those depths be shared with someone
else
Is it because now you have reached to another level,
Or just realized you're also like us, devoid of knowledge
about it.

Affable Amiable Words

In the span, words moved between us.. Some affable, some amiable..
Heard it all, remembered it all.. amidst the clamor, can now verse the tale..

Tale of how and where did the paths lay, how and where did the roads lead us to..
From the cradle to the end, all spoken and unspoken words we shared on the go..

We managed to stay afloat, holding on to the three words uttered during our roams..
Binding us, blinding us from the world while moving against the world, it saves us..

Do you remember our sane conversations? 'cause our friends declared us insane..
Do you remember others' pretext conversation? 'cause we really didn't care..

In hindsight, we have truly lived and loved our lives, said what we needed to say..
In the chaos, finding the peace, overwhelmed with the joy here we finally bid goodbye..

* * *

Venturing into Unknown

Are you afraid of the unknown?
Are you afraid you'd be lost?
Are you deep into the comfort zone?
To an extent that you can't match the cost?

Opportunities come and by,
Unexplored Experiences yell near you,
You in your street, your home, your chair,
Pulls you like a magnet, binding your movement due..

Aren't you afraid of missing on people, places, love, life?
Of not wandering enough, of not widening your horizon?
'I wish', ' I regret', 'I wanted to', the words that break you,
The comfort that blinds you, illusion you to the life of a con.

Remove the blindfold,
Pick a car, a train, a bus,
Get out of this place,
Turn towards bliss from curse!

I wish you bon voyage,
I wish you find your unknown,
The one which will fill that void.
Forever and so long!

* * *

Enjoy the Confusion

Being restless, I have been pacing back and forth,
In my room with the thoughts filled up in my head,
Drowning out the songs playing in the background,
Building scenarios, imagining the paths ahead.

Happiness and confusion with hand-in-hand,
Being carelessly happy or look for reasons high and low,
Trust the fate or anatomize the threads of incidents,
Can't decide, am I done with thinking through?

Some days, I'm taking the matters in my hand,
Feels like I can conquer my travels,
Other days, want to be a backseat passenger,
Love the way the road then unravels.

I know, I know, one day I will miss this scepticism,
These careless days, which I want to steer in my
direction,
Guess then I should listen to my intuition,
Love and laugh for now, enjoy the moment.

The moment with the starts and moon twined,
With the clicks and ticks in the conversations,
Diving and in motion with the ebb and flow,
Skips in the pace, admiring the nature's creations.

* * *

Lessons or Compulsions?

Do you also brood in the office when you don't have
work?
Because I'm sitting in my 8×6 cubicle looking at my
empty to-do list,
And I think to myself of the way the corporate life
wheels,
The more I am free, the more the corporate engulfs in
mist.
How do you respond when someone asks, "Did you
permanently move here? ",
I'm sure the answer will be 'Yes' or 'No', and then a
plausible explanation,
Wonder is when response is another question and
response to that is on another trajectory,
Lesson 1: No response is direct, concept applicable will
be "Create Confuse-ation".
You work and work and work for the review of your
department,
You mention the heading "Go-To-Market Strategy" and
get it reviewed by the manager,
And the heading is changed to "Market Entry Strategy",
that's when a valuable insight is gained,
Lesson 2: Don't mention Industry accepted terms,
replace "Go-to-Market" to avoid err.
You ignore the rest of the world and give your cent
percent to the task assigned to you,
Meanwhile, the small talks being made here and there,
with coffee or in the cabin,
Since you didn't partake in the "coffee" talk, you're not

working, probably playing games on laptop,
Lesson 3: If you don't take part in "employee engagement program", you will be talked in.
You did customer research, you got the root cause, long term results are confirmed
But what about the short term goals? Which one to go for? Short term for security
You disagree, you are convinced this will go for a toss, you are not working on the project anymore
Lesson 4: Disagree and you are dumb. Agree and hola! you stepped up rightly.
"You need to work on…", I saw my boss standing beside me,
The musings stops and now I'm back to the presentation version,
Work with all my sincerity and thinking about the lessons,
Tossed the lessons in the bin, plugged in earphone and be in introversion.

❋ ❋ ❋

The one. The trip.

Beach or mountain? Decide on one.
She pouted on the question.
She was a beach person, but
Occasionally she liked mountain run.

Well she couldn't and left to the group.
Rain. Wind. Trek. Settled for mountains.
With speakers blazing, snacks unraveling
The road trip, mountain trek began.

Rain. Rain. Rain. Trek is difficult.
Her mood sulked, well either the beach or…
Neither seems to be happening now.
Let's go around, better than doing nor.

First spot, hike to the dam, let's try.
Second spot, beach mountain combo.
Obviously not a beach, reservoir.
Nevertheless heaven to behold.

The feeling of being one.
with the wind.
With the earth.
With the water.

Significance of friendship. That's a lot.
Significance of love. That's a thought.
Black clouds and transparent water can do that.
Leaving you in tides of low and highs to be sought.

Cuddled in cold breezes, nuzzled in sparkling waters.
Seeing the colours merging with each other in layers.
It has to end. The moment has to pass.
This moment also passed, leaving me in trance.

* * *

Perfect Chaos.

D: "You know, it isn't easy.", the fingers dug further in the ground.

H: "What isn't? This, we being an escapist or realist? ", the eyes looked around.

D: "Why do we have to quit, if they don't understand? ", the thought plumbed.

H: "When you want to do right and being questioned absurdly…", the mind numbed."…it isn't quitting if you want to change the world but not allowed to, It simply means you being the bigger person stay out of senseless rue."

D: "Don't you wonder, what if, you would've tried one more time and made sense."

H: "Perhaps. Or perhaps you ought to create chaos, perfectly, as Je pense."

D: The eyelids lowered and a sigh came out, "Order cannot function."

H: "You need to leave them in chaos, for your sense of freedom."

D: Looking in the distant past, "I don't feel bad when I leave, but I do regret."

H: "It's not you questioning yourself, it is the memory of you in fret."

D: "I tried reasoning with them, reasons with reasons can be fought.."

H: "Exactly, but how do you convince with unreasonable belief they got"

D: "I can't surrender. But I refuse to be a pawn in the system."

H: Smile came on the lips which conveyed the depth of the understanding in them.
H: "You can see the order, you chose not to be part of it, you are a perfect chaos.
And that's how you will live for yourself, without on your shoulder an albatross"

You. Confidant.

You said you had a dream last night
I sat through the whole coffee to listen
You being the wind or the tip of the pen
Working your way up out of the prison.

You said you had thrown out of class
I called in sick and accompanied you
You being the free spirit breaking out
Brightening your smile by you true.

You said she broke your heart into millions
I hugged you and tried to cheer you up
You being the sword slashing the pain
Strengthening your soul and smiling at the cusp.

You said you didn't want me to go
I asked why you want me to stay
'Cause you came through and I will too
Not mere words, I promise, are they.

I said the words standing up there
You walked to me, saying the vows
I being your confidant understood
We were there for highs and lows.

* * *

Musings | Friendship

"What's the difference? You'll share your secrets with either of them.."

He asked, thinking of the unusual conversation that it's going to be.

"No, you don't. For starters, a best friend will be one and only one."

"Yeah, I still don't get the point you're trying to make here."

"If it is one, you are dependent on your best friend, vulnerable."

He looked at her expressions, he could sense what was about to come next.

He waited for a while for her to finish off her thought, not to stray from it.

"In that case, if your best friend hurts you or betrays you, you are devastated."

Ah! Here it is. The classic trust issue scenario, but finally I know.

"Okay. Then the scenario could be the same with a close friend, right? "

"No, that not might be. You see, you can have multiple close friends.

And thereby placing a certain amount of trust in them, expectations are less"

"Doesn't that boil down to your expectations? "

"How could you not expect when you give someone so much importance? "

"This implies that you don't give importance to your close friends."

She shook her head, "No, no, no, no, that's not what I meant.
It's impossible to rely on one person these days, giving them so much power.
Power to be your strength as well as your weakness, so you place that power in multiple people.
In that case, if you are hurt, it will be bad but you will have other strengths of yours to pick you up."
He looked straight ahead when she quoted the incident from history.
"Even Julius Ceasar ended up with his best friend betraying him.
So Basically there are some good or 'Close' friends whom you can rely on or trust on."
"To offer another thought to your musings, not every relationship is perfect"
"But you don't keep your hopes for those who have walked out.
You simply can't stop them, but you can rely on others"
"In that case you cannot trust someone else by giving your cent percent"
"Yeah, except in the case where you can manage your expectations.
Keep it to a minimum and live your life for yourself."
He looked at the sunrise and hoped for a new beginning here onwards.

✳ ✳ ✳

Little by Little

Little by little she cheered up,
Listening to music was her world,
The world to immerse herself in,
Words with which she will surround.

Little by little she started scribbling,
The lyrics which did her heart beat,
The support to draw her inner-self out,
To reach for the stars with a new start.

Little by little she painted the blanks,
Brightening up her canvas,
The charm to which she gave in,
For a smile that will last.

Little by little all said and done,
Living up to the ideal life,
The love that filled her soul,
For the journey to thrive.

Fear. Being Alive.

She looked down, 25ft below her feet,
The adrenaline rush, for what she has been looking,
Second by second, she could feel her heartbeat rising,
To catch that freedom, moment by moment fleeting.
Introvert in her said, "what the heck I'm doing, I love
my life, should have been a reader or a writer."
Extrovert in her said. "Can't wait to see what's next, I
love my life, I should have done it earlier."

She took a deep breath, inhaling and exhaling,
Too late to back out. Back out! I'm going to freaking
jump, thud!
"Okay, I like heights, but it is high! ", laughed an
extrovert at an introvert,
Few minutes of pure bliss, thinking she took one step
forward.
"I can do this", did the prep talk in her mind.
"What's to be afraid of, I love heights, I love water,
it's just a cliff jumping into it. Okay, push yourself and
lose the ground.
Loose the ground. Here I go. Here I go. Err."
"Are you ready? On three? ", the instructor looked at
me,
Of course he sees hundreds of people take a plunge
without second guessing,
"One.. Two.." without thinking she leapt forward with
knees in her hand,
Opened her arms and dived straight into water, it
breaking.

The cold water soothed her nerves and she emerged victorious,
Catching her breath and giving a shout out to others in joy,
She stayed reliving and cherishing that carefree world,
Alas, like everything, this will pass and will stay as a memory.
Smile. It has been a good day, with the chaos to follow.
Cherish. Memories pass faster than the shooting arrow.

✳ ✳ ✳

Princess Warrior

Yes, it aches, my heart aches..
not over a gentleman, but for a reason..
known as improper for a young lady..
to let go of the rein, to have a wild run..

To create history, not sewing or painting could..
To mount at the pace of gallop, a vivid imagination
would..

Pretty ribbons and a bonnet stuck on me..
Waiting for the gentleman to ask on the floor..
With a sigh I let my mind wander..
Writing novels, to look a new quest for..

Publishing my name in the hearts..
Copyrighting my stories in the charts..

"Doesn't suit a princess", they say..
The pages of my diary narrate a different cry..
Should I rebel or Should I give-in?
Write my own story, life has to wry..

"Keep your hands and chin this way, you'd be
introduced to a prince"
Without blinking, I let my eyes wince..

I shall be liberated, I turned towards the window..
Determined to give an apt ending to the story..
The looks of wrinkled paper liberated me..
Landed on the ground from the third storey..

"Are you princess? ", I heard the voice..
Run forever or face now, was the choice..

Turning around..
Resolution in some ways..
Fear in the heart..
Saw someone who slays..

Slays the society and its rules..
The prince indeed was not cruel..

I ruled as the princess and the author..
As the queen and the influencer..
As the mother and the advisor..
Published and copyrighted, signed my name as
'Warrior'.

* * *

Closed Spaces. Patience.

He tried to find his breath among the crowd,
Without making efforts, being swayed further and
further,
Closed spaces still bothering his psyche,
Would have stayed at home rather.

Checked his watch, the signal says stop,
Clutched his bag pack tightly and stretched his brows,
With the need to clear his head, he took a deep breath,
Conundrum of emotions, couldn't still the thoughts.

There has been countless things that was going on with
his life,
Which one to sort first and how to go about it,
Was the clue he had been searching for,
Being the optimistic he is, fate never questioned his grit.

"I might not have all the answers", that's what he ended
up thinking,
When looked around, saw crowd was still drifting,
Unable to hold his ground, became a dead log,
Sometimes it's better to be patient, than a rebellious
being.

Can't figure out whom to turn to for advice,
They are either in the same mind of frame as him,
Or trying to provide the solutions to lower his
satisfaction index,
Won't be settling for anything less, resolution brim.

Knowing well enough, the answers he is looking for,
Won't come before time, at some level he knows he

needs to wait,
Time that's the test he needs to ace,
Destiny is something which partially time will tell and
partially he will create.

Tale of Ambition

She moved around a lot and talks to strangers,
She got the reality check a while back,
Accepted the world as is and started managing her own
stars.

Scared? Confused? Excited? Cheered to face highs and
lows,
Move forward, don't be stuck in a place, being the only
motto
Keeping your eyes ahead, knowing let the bygones be
bygones.

People from past cropping up from time to time,
She reaching out to them, letting them reach her or
simply stringing along,
Being strong-headed and stubborn, appreciated the
honest crime.

Some days moved real fast and some days real bore,
Never forgot the reality check, never remembered it
though,
Met once again with the events, longed to go back, miles
abhor.

But she was not the same emotional wreck as she was,
Handled it gracefully, handled the stakeholders distance
apart,
But missed the hugs of go-to people, treadled through
the flaws.

The tale of ambition gives similar whirls every once in a while,
Think through it and sleep on it, and wear that beautiful smile.

Battle It Out

Sitting in a 2×2 box, he looked out the window,
in a quiet night, raises a voice deep inside his mind,
Long gone are those cards handcrafted by you,
From the attic, in the box earlier when he mined.

"I'm a person of future and not past", said out loud,
The rain drops on his outstretched hand said otherwise,
The voice inside his head laughed at his false virtue,
Conflicting him and enticing him in the web of lies.
"Doesn't matter what I think. What I do is."
The wind listening to it blew right past him,
Taking him with it to the land of childhood trips,
Seeing the faces and hills, Scrooge in him whims.
"You haven't won this battle. Quite the opposite,
With past and future, living in present presence,
Cherishing the memories had made and about to"
Voice, on victory, lopsidedly chuckled and went into
deep silence.

* * *

A Note to 25-Me

Dear 25 me, you are restless, I understand.
You are clueless and worried sick about your future.
You're wondering what's going to happen next?
Where would you be after a few days, few months, few years?
Yes, don't be surprised. I've been there, with those thinking nerves.
But I assure you, you're doing a great job so far, far better than I did.
Don't be so hard on yourself, give some time to let life take you.
Feed the right wolf, and it will take where you want to be.
Not everyone can handle mystery and history together.
Believe in yourself. Keep your passion up for life. I'll always be there for you.
I might not have all the answers for you, I might not give right advice to you.
You can, though still count on me, I will talk your worries out.
Yours truly, Self.

* * *

The Closure

I have been tossing and turning in the night
Thinking of what I could have said than what I did say
What said was because of this and that, with myself I bet
I sighed, looking at the clock, calculating how much
sleep I can get.

Click Instagram, Facebook, Twitter, Pinterest
Read some, Listen some, Like some, Share some
Being in Present in one moment, Being in Future in
other
Worrying in one moment, Letting go in other

Blinked twenty times quickly, trick I read about
Meditate to sleep, another trick I read about
Nothing seems to work, leaving at time
When night finally swayed me to sleep

Riding a car with people, people known and unknown
Having conversations for better or worse
These dreams related unrelated haunt me for a day
Go to line 1 till you find "the closure".

* * *

Done and Dusted

The world upside down, look at it from my angle
The three corners, we trio, form a part of a triangle
Worlds apart, opinions differ, goals at poles' length
Bonds formed nine years ago, shakes and strengthens
Daily talks, gossips, good and the trying times
That's not what defines us, there for each other?
No, understanding when to smack one's head
And listening so to make jokes and tease light
That's what we are.
Scalene is the image that sticks in my head
Travelling on utopian planet is our butter and bread
Hangouts once in a while, meetups when in town
Some things never change, and this is one of them
One chapter closes today, new one holds whatsoever
Have no clue, don't need one, no reassurances
Nine years does provide you a glimpse of a future
Some movements, some talks, are predictable
Certainty about uncertainty is a refresher for the trio
With love, hopes and dreams, I will leave trio at it
Cheers to new beginnings, new lives, new us.

* * *

Gray

I could see the colors fading into gray,
Clearing my vision, blinking the lashes for few more times,
I could still see the gray, VIBGYOR out of the sight,
Salt and water in the eyes gives away the crimes.

I tried to change the spectacles, from transparent to colored,
Not enveloping me were blue, red, green, but the gray,
I shut my eyes closed, hoping to see the blue thunders,
Alas, as my fate decided, I was bound to be a blank space prey.

Could anyone understand what I am saying?
Could anyone feel the torment I feel?
Surely no. How could a happy face see the sorrows?
How could an empty heart have moments to steal?

If something is still on your mind, do something about it.
Right, like fretting about it and keeping yourself shut?
That's an easy part to do, it doesn't make it better though.
"Wait, let this moment go", yeah move ahead with thrust.

"I finally found my way, say goodbye to yesterday"
Bon Jovi blasted at me, needing strength to slay the gray.

❊ ❊ ❊

Thoughts

The rose in her hand became part of her attire ..
The smile on her face became part of her makeup..
Minutes, hours, Days, weeks, months went by..
Her thoughts stopped the time and seized the moment..
'Time fades out everything' was the denial she lived
with..
Her happiness was the only thing she was living for..
Small talks, long talks and silence were something to go
by..
Friendship and love is a circle which never ends..
Time didn't fade anything, she changed with every
passing day..
Small talks were she living with, long talks being locked
up..
Silence soothed, keys being thrown away in the sea..
Circle might not end, the world could be flat..
Rose withered away,
Hourglass was the reminder,
Silence killed her,
Friendship and love were at the edge
Thoughts could play tricks on you..
Tricks of fine line between real and heart..
Roses shine or wither, smiles appear or disappear..
Hourglass is hers and hers alone to decide.

* * *

Hourglass

The post is a sequel to Thoughts.

The wet eyes kept on watching the sand and seeing it
slipping by,
Smoothly being mixed with its kind when her emotions
had been in turmoil,
The perfect picture was thrown off the wall,
From the memory there was no way to make it recoil.

Illusion shattered,
Rear-view mirror cleared,
Sun brightened,
Smoke disappeared.

Hold on to it or let go,
Fired were the arrows from the crossbow.

Rain, she loves.
Smile, she adores.
Tao, she walks.
Truth, she values.

Hourglass snapped her out of the thoughts,
The decision was hers and was made,
She turned the Hourglass upside down, let it go,
After all, what is about to change is her fate.

** * **

Mr. Demon

"Who are you? The one in hiding"
The shadow, growling, came out in the light.
"Why have you come here?, I demanded.
A deep voice replied, "to control you, to crush you."
"Nonsense! You have no business here."
I turned my back against him and started walking.
"I am here to imprison you. Surrender yourself! "
Encircling me he lessened the distance between us.
"On what charges, if I may know Mr..? "
"Demon", laughing in my face, he outstretched his hand
to grab me.
"Ha ha! You think I am afraid of you. Sorry to
disappoint you Mr. Demon."
I folded my hands across the chest and stared into his
eyes.
He took a step back but didn't lose his confidence.
"You will be. Aren't you aware of my powers? I am the
king of your world! "
"King! ", I laughed, "I didn't mean to offend you by my
laugh. Enlighten me, My Majesty."
"Don't you know that I reside in every human being on
this earth including you.
I master your mind, then your body, then your soul! "
"Is it? I've never heard of anything so incredulous.
Please don't let me interrupt you."
"You still don't believe me? But you do believe in fear?
Ignorance? "
"Fear? Ignorance? I don't follow you Mr. Demon",
perplexed I asked

"My sons. My pride. They both are indestructible. They empower me."

"Maybe. But what does that have to do with me? "

"I am here to live in your mind, you fool! "

"You've got quite a bit of humor. Fear of what Mr. Demon?

"Aren't you afraid of death? being poor? being alone? "

"Heavens No! ", seeing my confidence he took a step back.

"I think you are lying, which works in my favor. Lie is my pet."

"Lies are for cowards to say. I am telling you the truth and standing right in front of you."

Panicking, he growled, "If that is true, answer my questions."

"I am all ready for the test Mr. Demon", I smiled.

"Aren't you afraid of your loved ones going away from you? "

"If they are my loved ones, they won't leave me. Even if they do,

I am glad to make their acquaintance, they served their purpose in my life."

"Hmm, what about demotivation, curses, tears? "

"I used to deflect in my past, but I always managed to be on the right track.

Such words don't exist in my dictionary anymore! "

I could see the sweat beads on his forehead, so I gave him a smile.

"It is not possible! What about your decisions? Do you rely on the potential of your mind?

Don't others or the environment influence you? "

"No, Mr. Demon. The person whom you are talking about was old-me, which is dead.
This mind, body and soul belong to new-me, to optimism."

"I don't have leverage on you! How is that possible? ", he mumbled to himself.

"Sorry you had to waste your time Mr. Demon"

"Sorry? Politeness! Humbleness! Harmony! ", he growled, this time louder.

I turned around, put my cap on, and started walking away.

"How could you outwit me! What trick did you play?! ", he shouted in the background.

Singing to myself and swinging the stick, I enjoyed my path to calmness and peace.

* * *

Inspiration: 'Outwitting the devil' by Napolean Hill. Fear and Ignorance are our enemies. One needs to have a definite purpose or aim in life and a definite plan of action. One should always follow one's mind. One's mind and time are the greatest assets of all. Optimism, faith, and positive thoughts are the traits which show the right path. Always.

* * *

Hither and Thither

Staying up late, brewing a cup of coffee..
Staying up late, staring at a blank space in the balcony..
Staying up late, watching life going by..
Staying up late, one moment after another in the bay..

Bitterness teased my mouth..
Life teased my brain and heart..
Every day the routine follows..
Stay strong until two breaths last..
Where did I go wrong, considering all the ifs?
How would I have fared, considering all the ifs?
When would I have succeeded, considering all the ifs?
What would have happened if there had been no ifs?
If I had not moved here, life would have been better..
If I had listened to her, life would have been better..
If I had invested elsewhere, life would have been better..
If I had spent more time with them, life
had been better..
No one survived, harsh realities sinking in..
Nothing left, with life gambled away..
No one survived, comfort and love was misplaced..
Nothing left, my foolishness came with the price to pay..
Smiles I lost, tears I drained of..
Passion I lost, enthusiasm I drained of..
Dreams I lost, facing reality I drained of..
Love I lost, hatred I drained of..
You don't know how strong you are..
Until being strong is the only option..
They say. Laughing while carrying pain in the heart..

'Always smiling' should be your caption..
Last sip of the coffee, morning came by..
Last sip of the coffee, cold wind greeted the day..
Last sip of the coffee, a sigh whispered between the teeth..
Last sip of the coffee, staying strong before saying 'Goodbye'..

Identity. Mis-Identity.

I know who I am. I know myself..

I know who I am. I know why I wear that smile with the storm in my mind.

I know who I am. I know why I strive to be better than myself everyday.

I know who I am. I know why I am the way I am.

I know who I am. Put me in the center of the circle, I sure can steal the spotlight.

I know who I am. Put me in charge, I sure can boss the way out of it.

I know who I am. Put me with accolades, I will try to find something to learn.

I know who I am. Put me with artists, I will try to take the baby steps there.

I know who I am. The constant 'I's' defining my egos to the beyond.

I know who I am. Fitting in to bring intangibles to the tangibles.

I know who I am. Trying to figure out the role I play to make it meaningful.

I know who I am. Constantly trying to find something, not stopping to live.

I don't know who I am. Living in the future or past won't answer it.

I don't know who I am. Intangibles are as important to be in the mix.

I don't know who I am. Breathing the fresh air without answers is freeness.

I will find and cherish who I am, because only I can decide who I will be.

One Could Only Wish

Do you think if I write the word "religion", the walls
will prick their ears?
Will it inform different messiahs who will unite against
me to show the differences?
Or will it strip the wall down to the core to only realize
that something is not right?
One could only wish, One could only wish.

Do you think if I scribble the word "race", the
boundaries on earth will deepen?
Will it inform the leaders who will display their colors
with hands in their hands?
Or will it merge into one canvas to show how it makes a
beautiful landscape?
One could only wish, one could only wish.

Do you think if I utter the word "sex", the air will turn
into the storm waiting to brew?
Will it inform the unions who live by the code to protest
and show the importance?
Or will it open their minds to understand the one needs
the other, to complete the journey?
One could only wish, one could only wish.

Do you think if I whisper the word "capital", the
buildings will echo at a supersonic frequency
Will it inform CXOs to un-guard their offices to go
about nuclear solutions?

Or will it step down from its pedestal to be one with the ones to change the world for better?
One could only wish, one could only wish.

Letter to Love Dearest

Love Dearest,

I have strayed from the true path, admittedly many
times,
Me, myself has held myself back from the light,
You, you are my light and I have been away from you,
Because I was scared, I was, well, me.
I have spent so many nights thinking and imagining,
Shying away, shutting myself away from the true self,
Thinking that in the dream world, I would cease to exist,
I would not be me, but I will be with you.
I will hold you, I will be close to you.
Yes, when I open my eyes, when the reality hits me.
I know that I'm with myself, because I'm not with you,
I could feel you in the distant corner of my heart,
But I push you further down the lane so to be with
myself.

I know now that I was wrong.
I have been an utter fool to ever do that to you, to us.
Now I know, you're my light in those unfathomable
thoughts.
Now I know, you're the only elixir that could save my
from myself,
Now I know, being enveloped in your arms I can loose
myself,
To my true self, to disappear and fill you in my heart.
Now I know, what is it to be truly free,
Now I don't have to imagine or frisk away in my
memory lane,

Because I irrevocably want to be with you.
I want to leave away this world, knowing you are there
with me
I can now rest in peace, knowing you will my bundle of
joy
I can now leave the clutches of my past,
Hoping you exist in every inch of my being.

Yours, respectfully, Fear

Professional Journey

I have come a long way, from the time I decided that
this is the journey I want.
I decided it was upto me to make the path flat or my
favor of slant.

I crawled, I gasped for air, I punched the wall, I fought
nail and tooth,
How, you ask? I will tell the story, and promise to tell
the truth and nothing but the truth.

My boss (hereby known as butcher), bullied and tried to
control everyone's pee-schedule!
He shouted, insulted and dominated not just a junior
like me, but one of CXOs.
He made all of us cry, not just in washrooms, but out on
the open floor and bar,
If you don't think it as horrific, look from the eyes of
the 21st century who never saw war.

Obviously your recommendation will be to switch or
petition against the butcher snob,
But the journey I started on, I had to endure it until I
found another financially sound job.

It was not in vain, I got an insight about myself, I can't
handle difficult obnoxious buffoon,
And in the situation of fight and flight, well I fighted
while looking for flight options.

I believe in improving myself, I know I ran away from
the situation, but I got to know myself,

Did it make me strong? No, but I survived and I kept moving forward on the journey self.

I eventually did end up in the city which literally never sleeps and I was in awe,
Never being more than 200kms away from my home, I breathed life with no flaw.

I thrived, I stood in the spotlight, I dived into the cloud nine, I had my own fan base,
I did new and expensive city challenges, I did dine and went to movies alone,
But this did make me stronger, with the appreciation at work, I reveled ablaze,
But eventually good things become a norm and heart aches for the loved ones embrace.

I moved back to the home sweet home, which I left 7 years back with a sob
Finding myself loving the life I have carved for myself, and getting a new job.

Don't you want that when things are good, it should stay that way and you just stay jolly?
But by now even you know where it is heading, it did go downhill (only professionally :P)

I went to the new company, with new confidence, to take the world by storm,
When I reached there, guess what? Salaries weren't given for the last 6 months!
Why- God-Why? Disappointed and betrayed, that's how I felt, betrayed Si!

Because my boss, a friend at that time, with confidence hired me and chose to not tell me.

I just moved back, and I now have a job where morales are running low,
Everyone is looking out for new opportunities and to get out of this grim snow.

I literally was gasping for a straw! Luck favored me and in 3 weeks, I joined a new company.
Not my industry, not my strong suite, but being good at my work I built my brand easily.

Made some friends, shared some laughters, mastered my projects like back of my hand,
Then i started slipping into my comfort zone and the fact that learning isn't coming easy,
I need new challenges, need new projects, need to be up with my vision board,
Spoke my concerns, but alas it was in vain and decided to change the road.

I'm learning here, not work skills, but people skills and team skills,
The road till here hasn't been easy, but that doesn't mean I'm not grateful
I cherish all the ups and downs, they led me here after all to the core,
Made friends, Built my name, Learned from the best and most importantly, I am ME and more.

✳ ✳ ✳

L.O.V.E.

Love is difficult.
Love is not simple.
Love makes you laugh.
Love makes you cry.
Love takes your breath away out of happiness.
Love takes your breath away out of heartbreak.
Love will make you.
Love will break you.
Love will make you day-dream.
Love will make you lose yourself.
Love will bring positives in you.
Love will bring out the worst in you.
Love will sweeten your coffee.
Love will leave you with tears in your tea.
Love will make you toss and turn out of excitement
Love will make you toss and turn out of exasperation.
Love will make you survive.
Love will make you give up.
Love frees you.
Love gives you more responsibilities.

Love is difficult.
Can you handle the difficult?
Or take the life without love
Which will also be difficult?

* * *

Perfect

Perfect! Yes, that's how it is supposed to be.
In a painting, make those perfect strokes for the hair.
In a poem, make those rhymes perfect to feel it as a
poem.
In studies, get the first rank in class to be perfect.
In life, be the perfect person who knows the right things
to do at the right time
In life, be the perfect person who says the right things in
the wrong situations.
These are PERFECT dreams which are laid out.

Yes, this poem isn't perfect.
Yes, the painting I posted has disheveled hair
Yes, not always I ended up getting the first rank
Yes, I have messed up in the wrong situations.
And for a long time, the PERFECT tag reminds you
that you're pretending to be perfect.

That voice in your head, saying you have to be perfect,
that voice is imperfect.
That guilt in your heart, saying you are wrong to say
your heart, that guilt is imperfect.

Chasing this myth can become an obsession for one.
Trying to live up to the expectations can ruin one.

Embrace the imperfectness, that's what one is supposed
to be.
All the sunsets and sunrises aren't the same, yet all are
perfect
All the souls and love aren't the same, yet all are perfect

Own the imperfectness to find that perfect peace.
Live the imperfectness for the perfect life.

Ash & Ice

Ash: Hey, I had a dream last night and I wanted to stay in it forever.

Ice: Oh! Sorry to hear that, friend.

Ash: Why? Isn't this a good thing?

Ice: You wanted to stay in the dream, because you're happy there. I wish, you feel the same with your eyes open.

Ash: Who said I was happy in the dream?

Ice: (confused) But you said you wanted to stay in it forever. Why would you say that if you don't feel happy there?

Ash: (laughing) No, no, my friend. That's what I figured out in the dream. There's more to life.

Ice: Like what?

Ash: It is not about having happy days for every moment. It is about being accepted for who you are.

Ice: If you're accepted for who you are, you're always happy.

Ash: No, I still will face the sorrows, I will still cry when things are hard. I will still have mood swings and go into hyper-eating mode. I will still feel disappointment, betrayal and sadness.

Ice: And you consider that as a good thing?

Ash: It doesn't necessarily have to be a bad thing. I am ME. I don't have to hide the real me or pretend to be someone who I am not. When I talk to someone, I can talk without judgements. When I wear something, I can wear it without judgment. When I eat something, I can eat without judgment. I don't have to lie to get my way, because I am accepted for who I AM.

Ice: (thinking for a long time) Can you ever be 100% you in front of everyone?

Ash: Why do you want to hide yourself? If you have thoughts which you're ashamed of having, then you are not being authentic. You are manipulating, which again is not you and then with time it becomes a part of you.

Ice: To be honest, I can't even think how I will do that. When I keep myself in cubes and crushed, the world likes me. It makes me part of everything they like. I am treated as a valuable member of the gang. The moment I open up and share my thoughts on the glacier, they ignore and belittle me.

Ash: (sighing) I know. When I'm in a candle or in a gas stove, people hold me close and never want to let me go. The moment I open up and share the other side of me, they run from me and say names to me. They never accept ME.

Ice: They never accept ME too. I don't think the world is ready for that.

Ash: I know, I want to stay in the dream forever.

❋ ❋ ❋

Love Love

I love watching rom-coms,
I love sobbing to those cheesy lines,
I love seeing people falling in love,
I love the way the entire place chimes.

I love the story which fills my heart with warmth,
I love when Darcy is in agony seeing Elizabeth,
I love when with the insecurities Samson and Beyah
opened up,
I love when Evelyn Hugo finally confesses her love,
forward cometh.

I love to cry when they are not able to express,
I love to silently sob when they finally do,
I love the way heart leapt with joy in those scenes,
Because it's a reminder to myself that LOVE is always
true.

The one complaint I have, if I may,
The happily ever after is what they display,
I know the real life is far from it, that's why I watch it,
But they still raise my expectations to the zenith hay.

I love receiving flowers on a day with no reason,
I love breakfast in bed just for a surprise,
I love spontaneous gallivanting across the globe,
I love to cuddle on the couch with love cries.

I wait for the time when the fantasy and real collides,
Leaving me in awe and grateful for our lives,
Every morning is as beautiful as the sunrise,
Every night is as sweet as the moon lullabies.

* * *

Invisible

Do you know how it feels to be invisible?
Walking on the streets without anyone to greet,
Living under famous shadows, hiding on your own,
The doorbell rings, but none there for you to meet.

They say, if you want it, go grab it, dare to do it,
But I realise there are costs attached to it,
Now bigger question is - are you ready to pay the price,
If the answer is yes, ask - is it worth it?
If still you feel that it is - by all means, go and make your
destiny,
If you're hesitating, and can't handle things being south,
refrain from choice.

You have to be mentally strong enough to say,
Come what may - I won't look back, I will move
forward,
By all means - take that step and move up and towards,
If you're not sure and are still confused state
First make a decision - no one else can do that except
you
You, yourself, have to decide what you want to do.

Be in a shadow or make your own,
I will decide.
The circles I will move in,
I will decide.
The path less or more traveled,
I will decide.
To be visible or invisible,
I will decide.

* * *

9 789391 470227